HELEN KELLER

Helen Keller could not see, hear, or speak.

▲ Young Helen uses her fingers to read.

▶ Helen's father wanted to find a teacher for her.

2

Annie Sullivan was Helen Keller's teacher.

▲ Helen with Annie Sullivan

Annie taught Helen many words.

▲ Helen touched Annie's lips to "hear" her words.

What is Braille?
A young man named Louis Braille could not see. He figured out a way for people who could not see to "read." Raised dots stand for different letters and sounds. People feel the dots and read with their fingers. Braille is like a code. Here are the letters of Helen Keller's name in the Braille alphabet.

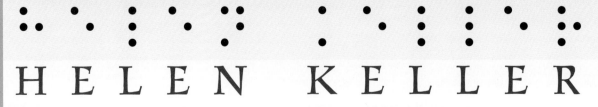

Helen learned that words have meanings.

▲ Helen reading a Braille book

Helen learned to speak and type her words.
She went to college.

▲ Helen went to Radcliffe College. She worked very hard to learn the things
everyone else did. She is shown here studying geometry.

Helen and Annie gave speeches and wrote books together.

▼ Helen loved roses. From the time she was a little girl, she would stop to enjoy how they smelled.

Both Helen and Annie wanted to help people have a better life.

Like everyone else, Helen needed money to buy food, clothes, and a place to live. She had many jobs. She wrote books, performed on stage, and gave speeches.

The 8th Wonder of the World
Helen Keller
IN THE PHOTO-PLAY BEAUTIFUL
"DELIVERANCE"

TOGETHER WITH HER LIFE LONG FRIEND, COMPANION and BELOVED INSTRUCTOR
ANNE SULLIVAN (MACY)
BOTH APPEARING PERSONALLY IN THIS MOST INTERESTING and INCOMPARABLE OF PHOTO-PLAYS
DIRECT FROM HER TRIUMPHANT TOUR OF AMERICAS BEST THEATRES

TREMONT TEMPLE || Commencing Mon. Eve JULY 19

Let's Explore!

Helen went to Perkins School. Look at the map. It shows some of the school's buildings. How could you get from the children's house to the head teacher's house?

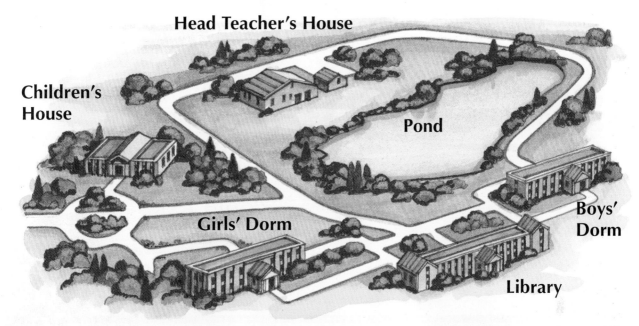

Head Teacher's House

Children's House

Pond

Girls' Dorm

Boys' Dorm

Library

Perkins School then and now

What Do You Think?

I Am a Star!
List some things that you do well. Put a star next to what you do best. Tell what you do well. Now, draw a picture of yourself being a star!

I Care, Too!
Helen helped many children who could not see or hear. You can help others, too. You could tell stories, teach games, or just be a friend to someone who needs one. Tell how you could help.

Pet Pals

Helen Keller loved dogs. From the time she was a little girl until she was very old, she almost always had a dog. Think of ways that pets are our pals. Draw a picture of your favorite pet.

10

The Braille Alphabet

a	b	c	d	e
f	g	h	i	j
k	l	m	n	o
p	q	r	s	t
u	v	x	y	z
and	for	of	the	with
ch	gh	sh	th	wh
ed	er	ou	ow	w

Helen as a young girl

Annie Sullivan

Helen and Annie

Helen with Alexander Graham Bell

Helen and Annie

Helen in 1915

Helen in 1960

Key Events

Helen Keller was born on June 27, 1880.

Annie Sullivan was born in 1866.

Annie Sullivan began teaching Helen Keller when Helen was almost seven.

Helen Keller graduated from Radcliffe College in 1904.

Annie Sullivan married John Macy.

Annie and Helen toured the world giving speeches.

Helen Keller wrote many books.

Annie Sullivan died in 1936.

Helen Keller died in 1968.